Damnée Manon, Sacrée Sandra

DAMNÉE MANON SACRÉE SANDRA

a play by Michel Tremblay

translated by John Van Burek

Talonbooks · Vancouver · 1981

copyright ©1977 Les Editions Leméac Inc.
translation copyright © 1981 John Van Burek

published with assistance from the Canada Council

Talonbooks
201 1019 East Cordova
Vancouver
British Columbia V6A 1M8
Canada

This book was typeset by Rosaire MacNeil, designed by David Robinson and printed in Canada by Hignell for Talonbooks.

First printing: October 1981

Rights to produce *Damnée Manon, Sacrée Sandra,* in whole or in part, in any medium by any group, amateur or professional, are retained by the author and interested persons are requested to apply to his agent, John Goodwin, 4235, avenue de l'Esplanade, Montréal, Québec H2W 1T1

First published by Les Editions Leméac Inc., Montréal, Québec. Published by arrangement with Les Editions Leméac Inc.

Canadian Cataloguing in Publication Data

Tremblay, Michel, 1942—
    (Damnée Manon, sacrée Sandra. English)
    Damnée Manon, sacrée Sandra

    Translation of: Damnée Manon, sacrée Sandra.
    ISBN 0-88922-184-7

    I. Title.   II. Title: Damnée Manon, sacrée Sandra.
English.
PS8539.R47D313   C842'.54   C81-091340-2
PQ3919.2.T73D313

Damnée Manon, Sacrée Sandra was first performed at le Théâtre de Quat'Sous in Montréal, Québec on February 24, 1977, with the following cast:

Manon	Rita Lafontaine
Sandra	André Montmorency

Directed by André Brassard
Set and Costume Design by François Laplante
Lighting Design by Michel-Pierre Boucher

Damnée Manon, Sacrée Sandra was first performed in English by the Arts Club Theatre at Spratt's Ark in Vancouver, British Columbia on April 19, 1979, with the following cast:

Manon	Clare Coulter
Sandra	Heath Lamberts

Directed by John Van Burek
Set and Costume Design by Alison Green
Lighting Design by Marsha Sibthorpe

Damnée Manon, Sacrée Sandra was also performed in English at Tarragon Theatre in Toronto, Ontario on November 22, 1979, with the following cast:

Manon	Clare Coulter
Sandra	Frank Moore

Directed by Bill Glassco
Set and Costume Design by François Laplante
Lighting Design by Robert Thomson
Music by Gabriel Charpentier

In her kitchen, which is completely white, MANON, who is very devout and all dressed in black, is rocking.

In her "dressing room," which is completely black, SANDRA, a transvestite who is all dressed in white, is doing her nails.

MANON:
The solution to everything. . . is God.

SANDRA:
It doesn't matter who, doesn't matter when, where or why, the answer is always to fuck.

MANON:
It's true.

SANDRA:
Especially not "why". . . "whys" are the worst.

MANON:
There's nothing you do, nothing you say that doesn't have God at the end of it.

SANDRA:
> Take me, for instance, I don't know why . . . about
> anything. And I don't want to know!

MANON:
> If you think about it, it's so reassuring.

SANDRA: *laughing*
> Why ask yourself why, it's stupid. Especially when you
> can fuck, so you don't have to think.

MANON:
> Sometimes I try to imagine something . . . I don't
> know . . . just some ordinary thing, or some big thing
> that's very, very important, that doesn't remind me of
> God . . .

SANDRA:
> Survival by fuck!

MANON:
> . . . and I can't find a one!

SANDRA:
> Survival by itself . . . impossible. It's got to be
> accompanied by something . . . something
> enveloping . . . and warm.

MANON:
> And I've discovered on my own, it's true that God
> exists.

SANDRA:
> I really can't think of anything but fucking to keep me
> alive.

MANON:
> And I didn't read all that in books, either. Oh, no, I . . . I
> just thought about it, by myself . . . with what little I
> learned in school. . . .

Silence.

Even if I'd never been to school, I'm sure I'd have come to the same conclusion.

SANDRA: *laughing*
Of course, not just any old fuck.

MANON:
Oh, yes, I'm sure of it.

SANDRA:
Nor any old piece of ass.

MANON:
I'm sure. . . because it's the truth. The only one. The only truth possible. And you just have to think about it a bit to discover it.

SANDRA:
Though at times. . . anyone will do the trick.

MANON:
And me, I've found the truth!

SANDRA:
When you get to the point where you'll take no matter what, then a fuck from no matter who will make you happy, no matter how badly he does it.

MANON:
God is at the end of everything.

SANDRA:
As long as it's still a fuck.

MANON:
God is at the end of everything.

SANDRA:
My God, you're crazy!

They both smile for a few seconds.

MANON AND SANDRA:
> Sometimes I ask myself, what did I ever think about before I thought of that?

> *There is a pause. Both characters are still smiling.*

> I can't remember. . . I was too young.

> *There is a long pause, as if both characters were preparing their confessions.*

MANON:
> I bought myself a new rosary this morning. . . . It's beautiful. It's splendid! It cost me a lot of money, but I don't care, nothing's too beautiful for God.

> *Silence.*

> I don't know if I'll say it before Sunday though. It's awful. . . I'm caught between two fires and I don't know what to do. . . . If I say it now, it won't count, because it hasn't been blessed yet and it would be like I wasn't praying at all. . . but on the other hand, it's so beautiful . . . and so heavy. I bought it 'cause it was heavy. I'm sick of cheap little rosaries that weigh nothing and look like nothing. I don't feel I'm praying any more when I've got one in my hands. . . . But this one. . . . When I saw this one, I was speechless. I was looking for a big rosary, okay, but that big! When I saw it, I thought to myself: "I don't believe it, is that a real rosary or an ad for one?". . . I was at the Oratory, because they have the best selection. . . and the most beautiful. So, I asked the lady if the big rosary was for sale. "Why, of course," she answered, "and I'm telling you, it works wonders! I just got it this morning. We've only been open an hour and already, you're the fourth person who's asked me. Isn't it beautiful? Oh, when I saw it, my heart stood still, no kidding. Do you know that the Mother Superior of the Sisters of Jesus and Mary, herself, asked the price! Of

course, we'd give them a discount, but it would still be very expensive. No, she'll probably send her chauffeur back to pick it up before the end of the day."

Silence.

I was so upset and excited when she said that! Then all of a sudden, even though it was huge, I said to myself: "I've got to have it! I can't help it, if I see someone else buy it, I'll be so disappointed, I'll. . .I'll. . . ."

Silence.

I think maybe I almost committed a sin there, just thinking that someone else might buy my rosary. Even the Sisters of Jesus and Mary. Just because they brought me up is no reason to leave them everything. Especially not my rosary. I was already calling it my rosary. . . .I asked the lady if I could touch it. At first, she said no, because she'd just hung it up this morning and she didn't want to spend the whole day hoisting it up and down. . . .It's so beautiful. "Not that I'm scared it'll break, mind you," she said to me. "It's solid. . .and I mean solid. It's me who's scared of breaking. The old ticker's been going too fast for some time now. . . .Oh, I do love God, but you know what they say, to adore Him and hang around with Him all day are two different things. I'm on my feet behind this counter the whole day. . . .I don't want to lose my job, you understand. . . .It's a good job. . .but they're pretty strict here with the ladies that work here." Finally, I offered to go behind the counter myself. Well, listen, I wanted to touch that rosary. She could see I was a serious customer, so she didn't stop me.

Silence.

It's red. Wine red. A beautiful wine red. And the crucifix is in black wood. Oh, it's so, so beautiful. When I touched it . . . even though it wasn't blessed, it's funny, eh, but when I touched it, I felt like something was alive inside . . . . It was . . . warm.

Silence.

The beads are half the size of my fist . . . and when you take four or five in your hands . . . they're heavy, and warm, and alive.

Silence.

I didn't even turn to the lady to tell her: "I'll take it." I had tears in my eyes. And I could hardly speak. I clutched the beads of a whole decade to my chest . . . and I took a deep breath. To keep from shaking. . . . The lady said to me: "You realize, it's very expensive." But I cut her off. "I don't care." I said it so fast that she jumped. Then I turned to her, as if to apologize, and very softly, told her: "I want it. Right away. I need it. Right away." The lady stared at me for a minute before she answered. It was as if she understood how I felt. Finally, she said: "Like I told you, I just got it this morning, so I still have the shopping bag. I'll go and get it." I took the rosary down myself while the lady went for the shopping bag.

Silence.

It's not plastic. No. Plastic's light as a feather. I don't know what it's made of. It's transparent, but it's very heavy. I can't figure it out.

Silence.

Maybe it's God's presence that's so heavy.

Silence.

When I'd gathered it all in my arms . . . I was so happy, I
didn't know what to do next. There I was, stuck behind
the counter with this big red rosary hanging all over
me. . . . I burst out laughing! I laughed so hard! I
laughed, I laughed! People were staring at me and the
more they looked, the more I laughed. Finally, I was so
weak, I had to lean on the counter.

Silence.

But I settled down.

Silence.

The lady came back with the shopping bag and the two
of us put the rosary inside. It barely fit! The lady was
amazed when I told her I'd pay cash. Her eyes as big as
saucers, she said: "Aren't you afraid to walk around
with all that money in your purse?" "Oh, no," I said,
"my Guardian Angel is with me and God's armed him
like a soldier to protect me from wicked people." Boy,
did she laugh. I always make people laugh with my
comparisons. I picked up my big package and caught
my two buses home. A little boy on the 129 thought
it was a set of blocks. But his mother told him: "Why no,
Raymond, can't you see, it's a big rosary. Look at the
nice wooden crucifix, isn't that lovely?" Then she asked
me: "Is it for a church, Sister?" I went all red. It's not the
first time that I've been mistaken for a nun, but it's the
first time someone thought that I was carrying things for
the Church! "No," I told her, "it's for me. It's my
rosary." And with that, the lady starts laughing like a
maniac. "For the love of God," she says, between a
couple of hiccoughs, "what're you gonna do with it, skip
rope?" Well, I wasn't gonna stand for that! "I'll have you
know, lady, rosaries like this are made for people like
you!", I screamed at her, right there on the bus, "for
people with near-sighted souls!" That shut her up. But

she didn't look like she understood. People can be so thick when they decide that they want to be stupid. Well, too bad for her! I didn't even tell her I wasn't a nun!

Silence.

But still, that doesn't solve my problem. I must admit, I'm a little embarrassed to show up at the parish house with my shopping bag to get it blessed. I should have had it blessed when I bought it, but I was too exited. I was too anxious to see how it would look in the place where I wanted to put it. No, I'll wait until it's blessed before I start praying on it. It's a sacrifice I'll offer to God for the sins of that crazy lady who understood nothing and who laughed at me on the bus. I'll pray for her on my little rosaries and wait to pray for myself on the big one.

SANDRA:
I know someone who's gonna cream his jeans tonight. Ah, and if he doesn't like it, he can go jerk off!

Silence.

I really don't know what came over me. . . . The things you do sometimes, it's weird. . . . You're just sitting around, as usual, doing the same old things, as usual, bored up the ass, as usual, not thinking about a thing, when all of a sudden: pow, flash! An idea! You ask yourself where on earth that came from. . . . Then you go on being bored up the ass trying to get it out of your mind. And you can't.

Silence.

That's what happened to me when I woke up around five this afternoon. I gazed lovingly on my splendid alabaster body, finding it a bit tiresome because I've known it for a few years. . . . My fine, supple little hands that shake a bit 'cause I smoke too much, but which are still full of life, knowing, experienced, perverse; my darling little tootsies, wide as a barge, that usually smell like a German shepherd, but which I always manage to disguise as a classy French poodle, trotting lightly but firmly around the bed; my thighs, too muscular for a woman, but which know how to loosen up when the time comes; my arms, ah! my arms; wings. . . . No, how can I say?. . . Feathers! And not ostrich, but swan's! My arms, downy before, steel wool during and merciless after!

Silence.

But especially, I gazed upon my superduper queen-sized dickie, so gorgeous, erect like a towering inferno, prepared like a boy scout in search of a good deed.

Silence.

If I didn't keep him in check, Dickie would help little old ladies cross the street! I said to myself: "You're aging well, old girl, you're aging well." No flabby folds on the tummy yet, the wicked fairy still hasn't touched your luscious thighs with her cellulite rod. . . and you're approaching the middle of your life. I'd even say you're standing on the threshold. Bravo, bravo, bravo! So, for my reward, I took myself on a Cook's tour of the premises, and paused lovingly at the most sensitive spots.

Pause.

Afterwards, I wiped my hands on the sheet. Well, all that's very nice, but there are times you wake up, eh, and even if you know you're still tempting, there's this empty feeling inside. . . . As if. . . something's missing.

Silence.

I got up to eat. Wof! Eat's a big word! I nibbled on a melba toast, with no more appetite than I chew my nails when I'm having my chimney cleaned by a trick with no talent. . . . What's more, my Nescafé tasted like chewing tobacco, never mind if I've never chewed the stuff, let alone seen it. Really, everything was all wrong. What do you expect when you have your morning erections at five in the afternoon, your life is upside down. Anyway, I found myself languishing in front of the mirror like I always do when I'm depressed. And that's when the lights went on. The minute I saw myself in that three-faced mirror that reminds me of all my friends, I don't know what I did. . . a look that I gave or a sweep of my swan's feathers. . . but it cut through my head like a meat cleaver: I saw my cousin Hélène when I was a little girl, though still a boy, standing at my Aunt Robertine's dresser, putting on green nail polish! To drive her mother crazy, I guess. Maybe she thought it looked good too, you never can tell. Anyway, she didn't get the idea from *Good Housekeeping* or *Châtelaine*. Not in 1952! I remember it was so ugly! Especially the green lipstick! Then. . . isn't it crazy. . . I felt like doing the same thing. Oh, it's hardly original, I know, fat Laura's been wearing black lipstick for three weeks because her Siamese cat that everybody hates was murdered with some liver pâté truffled with arsenic or old lace, or God knows what, by her own girlfriend, Jos Trudeau, who'd had it up to here with those two crooked eyes howling in his ear! But as for me, dressing up for the sake of dressing up. . . I don't like that. "Everything to turn 'em on, nothing to turn 'em off," that's my motto. But I had such a craving all of a sudden to do something crazy. . . . Can you believe it?. . . Green! Why green? I can't even stand a red the least bit deep, what with my capricious complexion. . . . I went back to bed and told myself it would all blow over. . . . Nice try, sugar plum. I could already see the look on my Caribbean siren's face when he caught sight of me with a green suckhole. A Mwatiniquais is vewy suspicious. He'd pwobably think I caught some tewible Wagnewian disease! "The Twilight of the Sods!"

She bursts out laughing.

"The Twilight of the Sods!" That's a beauty! I'm gonna put that in my repertoire! I doubt Cwistian would get it though. Anyway, I tried to go back to sleep; no way. I rolled it over on one side, then I rolled it over on the other, nothing doing. . . . By this time, I'm seasick, so I climbed out of my dinghy and jumped into my pants. "I can always try to find some," I said to myself, "who knows if they even make it any more?" Hoping I wouldn't find any, I stepped outside my palace of a thousand-and-one torrid nights and. . . . They had some at the corner drugstore! Mind you, this is no Tamblyn's. The owner is in her sixties, a jerk of an ex-priest, married to an unscrupulous travelling salesman. Which means that between the two of them, they'd flog their mothers for fifty cents and give you change. You walk in the door and pussy-face has dollar signs in her eyes and a bag marked "International Pharmacy" in her hand. But this time, I figured I'd plug her up proper, and not where you're thinking, 'cause wrecked convertible priests are not my department. I just said, like this, very matter of fact: "One 'Avocado Sea' lipstick please and a nail polish to match, natch." "Right away, Sandra dear," he says, without raising an eyebrow. How could he, he doesn't have eyebrows. And he pranced away behind his shelves of rat poison and other concoctions. I was, to say the least, dumbfounded. After two minutes and three seconds, this would-be has-been of a nun shows up with a tube of green lipstick and a bottle of green nail polish. They were neither Revlon nor 'Avocado Sea,' but they were green! And her, the sow, she was pink with pleasure! She flashed her aggressive dentures and cooed: "Do come and show me the effect." Effect, my ass! I could have shoved my fist up her Anus Dei, all the way to the elbow. But she wouldn't even notice, she's too used to it. I sure didn't feel like dressing up as an overripe avocado after that! A few shrimps and a Thousand Island dressing and I'd look like an entrée in a chic restaurant! Oh, but pride, what will we not do in thy name?

Silence.

I always assume responsibility for my actions, so here I am obliged to plaster my nails and kisser with green shit! I can tell already, the flies will love me tonight. But why do it if I don't want to any more. . . . Sandra, don't ask why!

She smiles.

Besides, maybe I still want to, just a weenie bit. . . . Just to see the incwedible look on Cwistian's face!

She bursts out laughing.

Never ask yourself why. Go ahead and do it. Life is too short.

She stops laughing.

As a matter of fact, it gets shorter every day. . . .

MANON:
I put it in my bedroom. I placed it in the hands of the life-sized statue of the Blessed Virgin. It's so beautiful, I. . . .

Silence.

I don't deserve such happiness. That's what I told myself as I walked down the street this morning. I had the shopping bag in my hand and I was so happy I almost felt guilty. When I turned the corner of the alley, I saw there were still some empty garbage cans that people hadn't taken in yesterday. One of the cans was knocked over, so I stopped.

Silence.

I think that's so dirty, garbage cans lying in the middle of the alley. Even if they're empty.

Silence.

I picked it up.

Silence.

And without meaning to, I glanced in at the bottom. There was an old missal stuck to the bottom, along with potato peels and carrots. A missal, in a garbage can. . . with the thought that had just gone through my head that I wasn't worthy of such joy. Right away, I thought, it's a signal from God. I knew it. . . . I didn't deserve my rosary. And God wanted me to sacrifice my beautiful rosary, so beautiful, that cost me so much, to help him save the sins of the world. My rosary had to go into the garbage with the missal. . . as an offering! It was a great honour. . . but so hard to do! My beautiful red rosary! And I'm not rich. . . . I saved up a long time to buy that! I looked all around. No one. I took a deep breath. . . . I didn't want to. . . .

Silence.

But there was the missal, stuck to the bottom. . . in the garbage! Someone else had already made her sacrifice!

Silence.

Slowly, I lifted the bag and lowered it into the can. I had to lean in.

Silence.

It smelled awful.

Silence.

All of a sudden, I burst out: "You know, God, sometimes You ask me to do the hardest things," I said to God: "But here, You're the boss, so take it." The bag just fit in the garbage can. I said to myself: "I guess that's where it belongs." Then I couldn't take any more and I burst into tears. I hadn't cried so hard for years. I leaned on the garbage can.

Silence.

I cried so hard my tears fell into the bag.

Silence.

All of a sudden, Mme. Quenneville's little boy, who I didn't hear coming, shouted behind my back: "So, you're a garbage picker now? You ought to be ashamed! You must be awful hungry!" And he burst out laughing. A real devil's laugh! I was so insulted that without even realizing it, I picked up the bag, shoved the little brat against the wall and ran into the house. I locked myself in, closed the Venetian blinds and threw the rosary at the feet of the Blessed Virgin in the corner of the room. "Your Son asks too much of me," I said, really mad, "at times, He goes too far. This rosary belongs to You. They always told us when we were little that every rosary in the world belongs to You, so here, take this one, too, keep it for me . . . and try to intercede for me please. I'm afraid that was too big a sacrifice for my little soul." I got down on my knees and touched every bead, one after another. Oh, not praying, it's not blessed yet, but I wanted to go over it once to see . . . just to see. And . . . that calmed me down . . . completely. In the time it took me to go once around, the Virgin Mary had settled everything with her Son. When I got to the crucifix, which I'd saved till the end, I wasn't sure if I should touch it. I said to myself: "If I haven't been pardoned, it'll burn me like fire." But I had faith. I put my hands close to Our Lord's body, I touched Him with the tip of my finger. It was just lukewarm. Like the rest. Oh, the warmth was still there, like in the store, but now it was even more comforting. The warmth of God, not the heat of the Devil. For a long time, I held my hands on the body of Our Lord who suffered so much for us...when all of a sudden...

Silence.

I felt this need...I felt this terrible need to kiss him....

Silence.

I couldn't understand...I had the crucifix in my hands and...

Silence.

All of a sudden, I started kissing the body of Our Lord, as if it were the last thing I would do in my life. I was sure I was going to die after...be struck down! What joy! What pure joy! Like bubbles of happiness bursting in my heart...and I could hardly breathe! I stayed prostrate for a long time. When I finally got up, I was completely at peace. I understood everything that had happened to me....

Silence.

God wanted to test me like He did Abraham when He asked him to kill his little boy in the story of the burning bush. God asked me to sacrifice what was dearest to me in the whole world and I did it! Yes, I did it! Like Abraham, I raised the knife against my most precious possession. I put God Himself into the garbage! And it wasn't the Devil that God sent to me, no, the Quenneville kid was His voice. My own burning bush! It was His way of saying, "You've done enough, Manon, go along home now and be happy!"

Silence.

I wish everyone could understand the workings of the world like I do. But most people don't know how to interpret the messages.

Silence.

Only a few of us understand.

Silence.

I hung the rosary on the hands of the Blessed Virgin and I got into bed.... The Blessed Virgin and I smiled at one another. Then...slowly...I fell asleep.

SANDRA:
I hope it smears. I wonder if they still make real lipstick that smears, like in the old movies. So kinky, to run my green lips over his black body.... What colour would that make? A lean sinewy body zebraed in green.... My God, I'm getting a hard-on! I can't wait!

She smiles.

One thing's sure, this'll be his first green blow-job!

She laughs.

I'm almost tempted to put some up my ass, instead of K-Y.

Silence.

They'd be right then, the ones who say I'm rotten to the core! A green anus! Sandra the Martian!

There is a long silence.

I'll ask him to stand next to the TV, naked. He's got these incredible buns. I'm gonna...I'm gonna open my green lipstick and write stuff on his back.... Every insanity that comes into my head. God knows that won't be hard. Secret graffiti, hermetic signs I wouldn't dare put on toilet walls for fear someone, someday, would recognize my handwriting and spread it all over town that "no one's as low as Sandra!" The shameful thoughts you write on your lover's back are the only graffiti that can really shock and besmirch those who come after you. Who would dare repeat a secret read on someone's back?

Silence.

Next, I'll draw circles on his bum, like targets. His cheeks like green targets with two black dimples. . . . Softly, I'll run my tongue between the two green targets. It will taste dark. I'll scrawl on his legs, his belly, his chest, his face. . . green signs that only I can understand. I'll write a pornographic book on his body. My own Bible. The Book of Genesis according to Sandra the Martian. The Pentateuch, the Song of Songs, the Old Testament and New Testament according to Sandra the Green. And above all, the Apocalypse according to me!

Silence.

Then I'll take whatever's left of my green lipstick, crush it in my hands and anoint his sex with green blood. My hands. . . will be green with sticky blood. . . . I'll stand back a bit and I'll say to him: "Open yourself wide and let me read!"

Silence.

Then I'll wipe it all away. I'll smear everything I've written to keep it for myself! Those who'll come after me are not deserving. I won't stoop to insult them. I'll rub. . . I'll rub until his skin and the green lipstick merge completely. I'll knead him, I'll oil him, I'll massage him with the green blood of Sandra the Martian. Next, I'll take out my cream-satin sheets, my beautiful sheets that cost me a fortune, that I never use 'cause they're too cold and too slippery. . . . I'll have him lie down on my cream-satin sheets. He'll be nailed to the middle of my bed. . . crucified with green glue. I'll close the sheet over him, drawing the four corners to his navel.

Silence.

I want to have a green imprint of the first Black God.

Silence.

I'll kneel beside the bed. If silence could invade the world! The street deserted, the television off, the radios dead, the babies bloated with pablum, the parents stuffed with chips and Coke, dozing before their own stupidity. To say nothing. Hear nothing. Only to wait. For the green of my blood to bleed from his skin into the cloth. Let it take time.

Silence.

Time enough to mummify him.

She smiles.

Yes, that't it, from now on, I'll mummify my lovers. All those who stick their noses in here hoping to stick their cocks up my ass will end up in the closet, hung up on hangers like old dresses we never throw out in case we lose weight again, or in case we put it back on. Dresses we know we'll never wear again, but we also know no one will ever wear again. No one will ever again go out this door to strut his triumphant virility in the small of someone else's back!

Silence.

I'm sick of being for them what they are for me . . . one among many. A number! A three-star fuck . . . or two-star . . . or one-star. A gourmet meal or a bowl of slop. Seventh heaven or the fifth basement. I want to be last. The last one to award the stars. The last one with the right to put the mark of quality on a piece of ass, like the stamp on a ham.

Silence.

When my collection starts taking up too much room, I'll turn them into lamps! I'll stick a shade on their heads and I'll pull their dicks to make them light up. Starting today, I'll electrify my lovers so they can throw a bit of light on the amourous thrashings of their successors.

She bursts out laughing.

We should teach our children to dream awake and out loud. It beats masturbation and it doesn't make a mess!

Silence.

When Cwistian gets a load of my unripened kisser, he'll probably get scared and turn tail like a rabbit. And I'll be left standing here with my greening plans. Unless of course, it turns him on and he throws himself at me before I've even time to tell him he's liable to end his days out on the balcony, stuffed with straw, with a turban on his head, a lantern in his hand and billiard balls in place of eyes.

Silence.

A beacon on my balcony, lighting the way to heaven for all the pilgrims in search of a fuck.

Silence.

Of the two possibilities, I don't know which I like best. Instant rape by Speedy Cwistian can be pretty humiliating, but he's so beautiful. . . . I think I'd rather look at him than fuck him. But I'm afraid beauty never lasts, even in green lipstick. Which means. . .thank you! Next! Maybe it's just as well he gets scared and runs. I'll take a last look at his fabulous ass and his legs long as organ pipes.

Silence.

Que sera, sera, eh?

Silence.

This green really is ugly!

Silence.

Hey, wait a minute, the clap is green too! My God, my lover's on his way here and I'm dressed like the clap!

MANON:

I had a dream. It's strange to say because usually I never dream. I read once somewhere that it's not normal, not to dream. That it's dangerous. But I don't believe that stuff. It never worried me not to dream. Dreams are bad. Dreams are something you can't control and things you can't control are bad. And the proof is: the dream I had this morning was bad. I must have been too tired. . .or too upset over what had just happened.

Silence.

And now, I'd give anything to forget it.

Silence.

If only I'd forgotten it the minute I woke up.

26

Silence.

I'll do all I can to forget it . . . but now . . . it hasn't been long enough yet. But I'm going to forget it! I'm going to forget it!

Silence.

When I was small, we had a neighbour who was crazy, hysterical, and she'd scare me. . . . A real maniac who'd do all she could to shock people. She was beautiful, but frightening, like a fallen angel. I think that's what she was: a fallen angel that God sent to remind us that hell exists and sometimes it's not far away. . . .

Silence.

I remember once I'd gone to ring their bell because I used to play with her cousin, Michel. . . . He was my best friend. . . . And she came to the door . . . I'll never forget it. She'd put on green lipstick that day, and I think her nails were green, too. . . . Yes, yes, her big devil's claws! I turned and ran back home, tumbling down the stairs. . . . I was screaming: "The devil, the devil, I've seen the devil!" My mother took me in her arms and told me it was true. That Hélène was the devil. We both got down on our knees and prayed for her . . . no . . . no . . . we didn't pray for her . . . we prayed to God that he'd get rid of her as fast as he possibly could. Her and her whole family? We hated them all, the whole gang! Except Michel. I loved Michel.

Silence.

I still hear her laughing, the demon.

Silence.

The demon with the green mouth.

Silence.

It was that laugh that came back to me in my dream . . . .

Silence.

I was lying on my bed, just as I was when I fell
asleep. . . I was still looking at the statue. . . Dear
God. . . will You never forgive me?

Silence.

Why did You send me that sign? Why have You upset me
even more than this morning?

Silence.

The statue's lips and finger nails were green. It was her.
Hélène. The fallen angel. With the same smile, the same
gentle smile as the Virgin Mary. . . but with her own
eyes. Those crazy eyes that would burn me when I was
little and she'd come down from their place and watch
us play, me and her cousin. "Not too close to the
balcony," she told us once, "you might be tempted to
crawl underneath and play doctor like we all did at your
age." Demon! Demon!

Silence.

In my dream, the statue was still clutching the rosary . . . .
But she held it . . . .

Silence.

It was dirty, the way she held it. They weren't the hands
of the Virgin Mary, held open like cups . . . . These hands
were closed around the beads. She was rubbing the beads
as she looked at me with her crazy eyes . . . . I started to
scream and the statue dropped the rosary on the floor.

Silence.

She came towards me. . . . I was so scared, I screamed!
I screamed! I screamed: "Vade, retro, Satanas!" Then
all at once, the Virgin Mary. . . no, not her, the other
one. . . Hélène. . . the statue. . . I don't know any
more. . . . The woman who's damned and all painted
green threw herself on me and she was saying things. . .
things. . . they were so gentle!

Silence.

Yes, it was gentle.

Silence.

And it was good. She touched me all over, just like I'd
touched the body of Our Lord, and she whispered to me:
"Do you like that, Manon? Do you like it? It's nice, isn't it?
Would you like to feel my lips on your body, all over, on
your skin, eh, like you were doing a while ago? You want
to know what He feels when you caress Him, when you
kiss Him? You want to feel how good it is? Eh?" I was
crying, I was pleading. She began to caress me all over!
"No," I said, "no, Hélène, don't do that, that's ugly! It's a
sin! It's dirty! That's not the way I do it! That's not why I
do it!"

Silence.

"I never did it for that! I swear it!" She stopped carressing
me and said: "I'm not Hélène! I'm not Hélène! Don't you
remember me? Don't you know me? We were the same
age. . . we were born the same day. . . we played together
in the yard in front of the house. I'm dressed like the rest
of them, but it's me. Don't you recognize me?" For a
second, I took him in my arms and held him tight, tight,
tight. . . .

Silence.

Michel! Michel! Why did you become like her? She was
crazy! Look what you've become! A degenerate!

Silence.

She screams.

Why have You done this to me? Why so much in one day? Why do You put him back on my path, that little boy I loved so much and who's followed his sick cousin into hell! Why didn't You send me a dream filled with Your presence instead of that other one? Why were her caresses so good for me? It's for You that I sacrificed my life! My whole life!

Silence.

She speaks very quietly.

When I woke up, I was soaked with sweat. And . . . . Oh! The statue was in its place, but the rosary was on the floor. One of the hands was broken.

Silence.

And You know how much I believe in signs! In the signs You so often send to comfort me, to test me, or sometimes just to remind me You're still there, beside me, omnipresent . . . beneficent . . . protective . . . fatherly! If You start sending me signs I don't understand . . . .

Silence.

She speaks louder.

If You start sending me signs *I don't want to understand,* I'm warning You, You won't fool me! I will not understand them! If You get too demanding, just remember, I can make demands too! I believe in You because You exist, but also I believe in You because You're good! Because You have to be good! The dream You sent me today wasn't good! And I'm sending it back! You made me commit a sin while I was asleep . . . . You hear me? . . . I was asleep!

She screams.

I couldn't defend myself!

Silence.

I'm sorry. Perhaps You're right. I'm sorry. Forgive this poor soul. . . this poor lost soul. . . a poor confused soul. . . . Forgive me. Forgive me.

Silence.

Take me back. Back to Your heart. Take me back. Take me back. Take me back to Your heart.

SANDRA:
Sometimes it just comes over me. . . . Doesn't matter what I'm doing, I have to drop everything. Just before I plunged into my green paint a while ago, it hit me. . . . And when it happens, it's pointless to try to resist. I ran to my mirror, took off all my clothes and slopped my puss with make-up remover. . . . I scrubbed and scrubbed, I think I used up two boxes of Kleenex, Man Size. I wiped my face completely away. I pulled my hair back with an elastic.

Silence.

I have the honour to officially declare that of the man I was not a single trace remains. Nothing! However much I looked, dug, examined. . . I could not find myself. My own face has ceased to exist. Completely vanished beneath the tons of make-up to which I have subjected it, vanished behind the dozens, the hundreds of other faces I've drawn in its place. . . . When I remove my make-up, my eyes disappear, my mouth shrinks, my eyebrows move, my cheeks puff up. . . and none of it goes together. The hundred other faces of women that I've drawn, that I've created myself, look more like me than what's left underneath.

Silence.

To find myself naked in front of a mirror, exactly as Mother Nature created me, gives me vertigo of nothingness. I don't exist any more.

She smiles.

The only thing that's still me . . . the only thing that's still the same . . . oh, it's matured well, 'cause it's hung around so long . . . it's grown in experience, 'cause it's lived life to the hilt, it's even been forgiven for having loved too much . . . the only thing I've never disguised . . . that's right, is my cock. Its appetites are the same, its demands are the same, even its illnesses, little head colds or serious diseases, the shameful ones, the runny ones, the ones that give pimples, they haven't changed. I have . . . remained my cock. The rest is only accessory. The rest is fabrication, an invention to lure into a thousand nameless traps the thousands of victims my cock is lusting after with his appetites voracious and his instincts ferocious. I'm not a woman by taste, I'm not a woman by need. My cock is merely a piece of go-between meat at the service of a gluttonous crotch! My cock commands; me, I obey! A slave? Of course! Such a beautiful word. Full of promise. Lies. Cunning. Twists. But at times, enormously gratifying. I am the slave of my senses.

She bursts out laughing.

When I'm neither on the prowl nor fucking, I'm not alive. The rest is filler. Everything I'm saying now is filler. Between my Martiniquais this morning before he went off to work and my Martiniquais tonight when he gets home from work. Me, I'm for action! No words. Pure. Speech is a venomous act, but fucking is a stream of honey flushed out from under cover, spread out in bright sunlight and savoured in the white burst of silence.

There is a long silence.

I found my masquerade for today. While doing my first nail a while ago, I found the face that the variable Sandra will don tonight. I have decided it will be the Virgin Mary herself who will receive a Martiniquais in her bed tonight. A new role. A new composition. The Mother of us all. To play the role of our Mother in the arms of the ascending race. To submit oneself to the Black, to yield to Him, sacrifice to Him, the purest, the most sacred image of our degenerate civilization.

Silence.

I'm gonna dress up like the life-sized statue that screwball next door bought after a fire destroyed part of the church in our parish. A statue bought in a fire sale. What an image! It's the statue of the Virgin Mary picked up in a fire sale that will get it in the ass tonight with the gigantic wang of the victorious Martiniquais! I'll stand in the corner of my room in my white dress, my blue cape and my little gold belt. . . . Yes, I'll stay standing the whole time! He'll lift my dress from behind. I won't move. My arms open. The frozen smile. But green! My eyes fixed, empty, turned in upon the ravaged saint. Saint Sandra the Green of the Fire Sale!

There is a long silence.

I am the Immaculate Cuntception! And it's tonight the Black Sparrow of the Holy Ghost will pay me a little visit. . .to bring me the Big News. . . . And the Big News is that the New Messiah will be one very weak baby!

MANON:
I have always followed Your instructions to the letter. Even if it meant great sacrifice. And You were never too shy about asking for those! I saw You at the end of all my suffering because You made me realize that You were present everywhere and I accepted every misfortune with pleasure *in order to be with You!*

Everything in my life centres on Your presence! I wanted to become a nun at one time. You didn't want me to, so I didn't. I hope You remember at least. When I was a teenager, that was my greatest wish, my most beautiful dream. To take Communion with the other nuns in the infinite pleasure of Your presence. And there was nothing to stop me. . . . I was all alone here, my mother and father were dead. . . and my sister. . . .

Silence.

My mind was almost made up when You forbade me to do it. Do You remember that afternoon? You told me Yourself, inside me. You softly, but firmly murmured in my ear that my place wasn't there, but here. In my mother's bed, in my mother's life. . . . You ordered me to perpetuate my mother who was a saint. . .even though it cost me dearly, even though I cried for days, because, for me, the convent was the very picture of happiness in communion with You. . .even if *I* thought I belonged in a convent, I stayed here for You! You've given me ample compensation since, that I won't deny. . . . For fifteen years, You have given me enormous joy and my gratitude is even greater still. . .but. . . .

Silence.

She speaks softly.

You don't come to see me so often any more. I don't feel Your hand on my hand or on my head like before. . . . Now, I need ten times the energy, ten times the concentration to finally feel Your breath in my soul. Before, I had only to think of You and Your breath would carry me off. You'd come right away and the two of us would smile and float away, leaving everything behind us, You, Your golden throne where a crowd of saints, each more important than the other, waited on

You, prostrate, passive, submissive... and me, my rocking chair, with my potatoes to peel and my carrots to shred. It didn't take two seconds, then hours would pass and neither of us would even notice.... You said so Yourself!

Silence.

Entire days we'd spend together between heaven and earth, while You'd explain the world to me in a way I could understand and forgive it, and I'd listen to You, on the verge of fainting. And I'd tell You that everything that You do is done well, that You are perfect, and that I must have been the luckiest person in the world to have found You. You made me happy, perfectly happy for fifteen years!

There is a long silence, then she explodes.

I have a right to my pleasures! I have a right! I'm used to them now! I like what You did for me and I want it to continue! You don't just ask a poor girl to sacrifice herself for fifteen years and then drop her! I have to coax You now with rosaries the size of watermelons and go through your Holy Mother in order to reach You. Does that seem right to You? And again, today, I still haven't succeeded. I haven't felt Your presence for a second! It's the first time that's ever happened!

Silence.

Can't You see I need You? I'm on the verge of blasphemy. If one day goes by, one single day, that You don't come to see me, I'm warning You, I'll go crazy and then I'll be capable of anything! I know, lately I'm tired sometimes... it's hard for me to met You halfway... but couldn't You make a little effort? I sincerely believe You are everywhere at all times, but that little bit of Yourself You give to me alone, what's become of that? You've given it to someone else. A new soul who's fresh and more available... already! No, that cannot be! You can't cheat me like that, walk away as if You didn't need me any more! If. . .if You abandon me, I'm capable of plenty, you know! If You abandon me, Satan is not far away and I could easily go find him myself, before He even thinks of throwing himself at me!

Silence.

If You don't come right away, I'm lost.

Silence.

It wasn't You. I know it wasn't You who sent me that dream a while ago. . . .You know as well as I do there's a part of me that would like nothing better than to throw itself head first into the great abyss! So make up Your mind! It's Your choice! Me, I let myself go! It was always You who made the decisions, don't stop now. It was always You who took my fate in Your hands, so I'll tell You once and for all, it's Your responsibility! I wash my hands of it and if I lose myself, then it's You who loses me!

There is a long silence.

She closes her eyes.

Ah!. . .Ah. . .yes. . .finally. . .I feel it. . . .

She smiles.

I feel You coming. . .yes, yes, closer. . .come closer and I'll forgive You for everything! Oh, for the love of me, where were You? I gave You my life. . .give me my share of Yours! Haaa. . .yes. . .take my hand. . .take me away. . . .

SANDRA:

When I finish my nails, I'll go sit on the balcony
and wait for Cwistian. I'll keep doing my number,
perpetuate my role of comic transvestite for all the
neighbours who must already be waiting for me,
wondering what I'll come up with today.

Silence.

They accepted me pretty fast around here. . . without
ever knowing who they were dealing with.

There is a long silence.

I moved back to Fabre Street right across from the house
where I was born.

Silence.

When I saw the ad in the paper two years ago, I couldn't
believe my eyes. A sign from heaven! I trotted right over,
disguised as a quiet, young stenographer, yet another of
my dazzling compositions. The landlord never had a
clue, my handwriting's illegible! So. . . ever since then,
I've been watching Fabre Street live, all over again. I
returned to my task.

Silence.

In no time at all, I was friends with most of the women.
Of course, they knew right away I wasn't a real woman.
They'd never seen a number like me up close.

Using different voices.

"How do you do it?" "Why do you do it?" "Did you have
an operation?" "Don't ever let me catch you sniffing
around my husband!"

Silence.

What they don't know is that this variable woman, this character who's so funny and so original, who they've grown used to seeing wiggle down the street with men of all ages, all conditions, all colours and all beautiful . . . is little Michel who lived in the house across the street twenty-five years ago. For some of them, a childhood friend, the baby of that crazy family of twelve, all piled into the same house, that made so much racket for everyone else.

Silence.

It's incredible how little Fabre Street has changed. Just aged a bit. But not changed. Not at all. At least half my childhood friends, especially the girls, have stayed here, married here and had kids that look like us. At times, it's as if I can see our gang playing out there in the alley . . . while the girl next door, with whom I played doctor a quarter century ago, knits beside me as she tells me things I know almost better than she, about her childhood, which, by the same stroke, is also mine; our games, our joys, our boundless happiness to be small in the fifties . . . and noisy . . . and Masters of the World!

Silence.

To have been a child on Fabre Street is a privilege that leaves an indelible trace.

Silence.

I suppose it's the same for everyone else, except I wasn't there.

Silence.

Obviously, no one recognized me, but most of the girls came back to me, like before, to tell me their troubles, saying afterwards, without fail: "You really understand us, don't you, us women?"

Silence.

Yes, I do.

Silence.

Now they say: "It's because you're queer," while before they'd say: " 'Cause you take the time to listen to us."

Silence.

To think that that's when they were right.

Silence.

Sometimes I want to come right out and tell them: "Hey, it's me, look, remember me? I was the leader of your gang! It's me who organized the picnics at Parc Laurier and Parc Lafontaine. It's me who made myself a Batman costume and haunted the alleys at night to scare you. If only you knew. If only you knew how it's me who was scared. I pretended to be brave and you thought I was brave. I pretend to be a woman and you think I am a woman. I've always fooled you because I had to, but if you only knew. . .if you only knew how much I love you!"

Silence.

But I would never tell them that.

Silence.

There's only one of them I've never dared speak to again. . . .When I first saw her. . .I'd just moved in that morning and I'd decided to eat on the balcony, 'cause the house was a mess. I saw her turn the corner, all bundled up in her old maid's outfit, her hair pulled back, her eyes to the ground, looking at the tips of her shoes, her little waddle of a walk, like an embarrassed nun. . . .Manon. . . .Manon, my sister. . .my twin. . . .

Manon, who was born the same day as I, almost to the hour, to whom I gave all the passion I possibly could; her twin, born of a different mother, but exactly like her. . . . Manon, my antithesis, my contrary, forever clinging to her mother's skirts, a false saint, dry as a prune, while I gravitated around my enormous mother, generous to a fault, suffocating as a dog day. . . . Manon, whom I would like to have taken in my arms, to kiss her, caress her and say: "What has become of you. . . . Look at me, I'm the shame of society," laughing and clapping my hands.

Silence.

But. . . the minute I saw her, I knew she was impregnable, inviolable, inapproachable, smooth as a stone, slippery as moss, cold as an ice-floe. Impossible to touch. Like her mother. When her mother would see me, she'd say: "That child is a sin!"

Silence.

For two years, I've watched Manon dry up like a raisin and I've never, never dared speak to her. She doesn't know I'm here. My mere presence would kill her. I am the negation of her life.

Silence.

Of her Faith.

Silence.

If what people tell me about her is true and it probably is true — she's my twin, I feel her, I know her, she's me — if all that is true, I envy her! People who are happy are so rare.

She laughs.

When I feel like crying, I go and stick my nose to the window and stare at Manon's closed Venetian blinds. Sometimes a faint little light, yellow, almost dirty, sneaks out through the metal strips, the bars of her prison. The light of a flickering candle. The light of a dying heaven and a rising hell. And I tell myself: "Manon has just left on one of her long journeys towards day."

Silence.

I have found someone truly happy whom I can watch live her happy, mouse-like life, surrounded by the decor of my own happy childhood. And I am reassured. About everything.

Silence.

If Manon had not existed, I would have invented her.

MANON:
My head has wings. My mind is like a bird cage with the doors wide open. All my thoughts fly out of me at once. Like sparrows set free. Everything flows from me. I am emptying out, I destroy everything in my path. My thoughts pulverize Fabre Street and I stand amidst the ruins like a rising spring. . . . Not too fast! Not too fast! Too fast is no better. Don't take me too high, too soon. Wait for me! If I get dizzy I'll fall and I'll have to start over!

Silence.

Ah! I've found my wings again! I'm soaring! In Your vast shadow! You shield me from the sun because its light is evil. Only Your light which seeps into the darkest night, the most secret shadows, which tears the soul as blows from a sabre, pierces the eye, bursts it, opens and revives it, only Your light which bites the skin and leaves the mark of wounds, only Your light which explodes the truth, the only truth, Your truth, only Your own light is good. The only one possible. The only one liveable. You have humbled Yourself to give me an infinitely small particle of it, which kills me. Your truth crucifies me. I find, at last, supreme joy in Your shadow, sheltered from all defilement. I follow You like a speck of dust, yet I glow like a comet.

Silence.

I am . . . a speck of gold dust in the eye of God!

Silence.

Ah! Higher! I'm ready now! Higher! Crush me beneath Your weight. Make of me a thing deformed, twisted, but holy; let me limp in the fringe of Your will!

Silence.

Let me obey!

Silence.

Give me Your hand, I can't see You now. I can't feel You any more! Don't leave me like this, alone in the void. I feel like I don't exist.

Silence.

Hurry, come take me, I feel that I only exist inside someone else's head! Don't let me fall back. If I do, it's not my own body I'll find. If You let me fall, my lips and my nails will be green. Help me! Help me deny my body! As long as possible! Give me back my wings! Give me back my wings, I'm falling!

She screams as if she were falling.

Ah!

She opens her eyes and bursts into tears.

What have I done to be punished so! What have I done to be punished so! Take me back with You, You are all I have left in my life. You are the answer to everything...in my life! I've destroyed all doubt...my faith is all I have left. All I have left are the rewards offered by my faith in You. All I have left are the rewards I offer myself for my faith in You. I believe in You. So You believe in me! Even...if...I have... been...invented...by...Michel.

SANDRA:

Go on, Manon...climb!

MANON: *as if she were flying away*

Ah...ah...thank You! I knew it! I knew it! Thank You, dear God! Thank You!

SANDRA:

Climb...higher...climb!

MANON:

Yes...higher!

SANDRA:

Keep going...right to the end! Go to the end of your journey! Climb! Climb! Climb! And take me with you! I want to leave!

She screams.

Take me with you, because I don't exist either! I, too, have been invented! Look, Manon! Look! His light is coming!

There is very intense light for five seconds, then a blackout.

Colours in the Dark - James Reaney
The Ecstasy of Rita Joe - George Ryga
Captives of the Faceless Drummer - George Ryga
Crabdance - Beverley Simons
Listen to the Wind - James Reaney
Esker Mike & His Wife, Agiluk - Herschel Hardin
Sunrise on Sarah - George Ryga
Walsh - Sharon Pollock
The Factory Lab Anthology - Connie Brissenden, ed.
Battering Ram - David Freeman
Hosanna - Michel Tremblay
Les Belles Soeurs - Michel Tremblay
API 2967 - Robert Gurik
You're Gonna Be Alright Jamie Boy - David Freeman
Bethune - Rod Langley
Preparing - Beverley Simons
Forever Yours Marie-Lou - Michel Tremblay
En Pièces Détachées - Michel Tremblay
Lulu Street - Ann Henry
Three Plays by Eric Nicol - Eric Nicol
Fifteen Miles of Broken Glass - Tom Hendry
Bonjour, là, Bonjour - Michel Tremblay
Jacob's Wake - Michael Cook
On the Job - David Fennario
Sqrieux-de-Dieu - Betty Lambert
Some Angry Summer Songs - John Herbert
The Execution - Marie-Claire Blais
Tiln & Other Plays - Michael Cook
The Great Wave of Civilization - Herschel Hardin
La Duchesse de Langeais & Other Plays - Michel Tremblay
Have - Julius Hay
Cruel Tears - Ken Mitchell and Humphrey & the Dumptrucks
Ploughmen of the Glacier - George Ryga
Nothing to Lose - David Fennario
Les Canadiens - Rick Salutin
Seven Hours to Sundown - George Ryga
Can You See Me Yet? - Timothy Findley
Two Plays - George Woodcock
Ashes - David Rudkin
Spratt - Joe Wiesenfeld
Walls - Christian Bruyere
Boiler Room Suite - Rex Deverell
Angel City, Curse of the Starving Class & Other Plays - Sam Shepard
Buried Child & Other Plays - Sam Shepard
The Primary English Class - Israel Horovitz
Mackerel - Israel Horovitz
Jitters - David French
Balconville - David Fennario
Aléola - Gaëtan Charlebois
After Abraham - Ron Chudley
Sainte-Marie Among the Hurons - James W. Nichol

The Lionel Touch - George Hulme
The Twilight Dinner & Other Plays - Lennox Brown
Sainte-Carmen of the Main - Michel Tremblay
Damnée Manon, Sacrée Sandra - Michel Tremblay
The Impromptu of Outremont - Michel Tremblay

TALONBOOKS — THEATRE FOR THE YOUNG

Raft Baby - Dennis Foon
The Windigo - Dennis Foon
Heracles - Dennis Foon
A Chain of Words - Irene N. Watts
Apple Butter - James Reaney
Geography Match - James Reaney
Names and Nicknames - James Reaney
Ignoramus - James Reaney
A Teacher's Guide to Theatre for Young People - Jane Howard Baker
A Mirror of Our Dreams - Joyce Doolittle and Zina Barnieh